BARNYARD STORIES AND POEMS

A Story Book/Coloring Book

For Pre-School & Elementary Grade Children 3 to 7 years old

By Artie Kaplan

Illustrations by Joe Toto

ISBN: 978-0-7596-1693-6 (sc)
ISBN: 978-0-7596-1692-9 (e)

Print information available on the last page.

This book is printed on acid-free paper.

1stBooks - rev. 11/7/19

Buzzy Duck's Wonderful Discovery
Charlie Chicken's Great Adventure
Billy And Bobbie Beavers Trip To The Summertime
Pattie Pig Loves To Eat
The Dreams Of William Goat
Billy's Red Wagon

Written by Artie Kaplan

5 Poems Coloring Book

One Little Green Frog
Two Little Honey Bears
Three Little Bunny Rabbits
Four Little Kitty Cats
Five Little Ducklings

Written by Artie Kaplan
Illustrated by Joe Toto

Where Is Farmer Jones?
Coloring Book

Written by Artie Kaplan
Illustrated by Joe Toto

First edition 2000

Book Designed by Valerie Kennedy

CONTENTS

INTRODUCTION

This book contains six original stories and six poems by Artie Kaplan with illustrations by Joe Toto.

It is designed to make young children aware of traditional values.

Before reading the enclosed stories, the teacher or parent can ask the children to look and listen for something specific as it pertains to traditional values.

At the conclusion of each story the teacher or parent can have a discussion with the youngster about the importance of these values and how these values can effect their lives.

For very young children, with short attention spans, the teacher or parent can read each story and point out the lessons to be learned.

By doing so, the teacher or parent will help children develop an understanding for the importance of these values.

An audio CD of the author reading the enclosed stories and poems is available for this book. Consult our websight at: AKPRecords.com, email us at: awk@.airface.com
or write for a price list to: AKP Inc., PO Box 4008, Deerfield Beach, FL 33442.

BUZZY DUCK'S WONDERFUL DISCOVERY

As the sun began to rise through the early morning mist, all of the animal families were waking up to start a brand new day. The barnyard was buzzing with activity.

Momma Duck and her five little ducklings were out on the pond bright and early. She wanted to make sure that they all learned how to swim before she allowed them to go down to the water by themselves. Buzzy Duck, Wuzzy Duck, Duzzie Duck, Cutzie Duck and Bootzie Duck paddled right behind Momma Duck.

"This is really hard work," said Buzzy Duck, trying to keep up with the others. "I'd rather stay in bed than do this. Why do Ducks have to swim anyway?" asked Buzzy.

Cutzie and Bootzie just giggled. Buzzy was being so silly. They all understood what Momma Duck was doing. Momma didn't blink, she just turned her head around, looked at Buzzy with a gleam in her eye, and said, "Now Buzzy, who ever heard of a duck who stayed out of the water? If you don't learn to swim like your brothers and sisters, you're going to wind up scratching around the barnyard all day with the chickens. Just keep on paddling until you get the hang of it and you'll be ok."

"Yes Momma," said Buzzy, "but I really don't understand why I have to learn how to swim." Momma Duck was very patient. She knew that Buzzy had to learn to swim.

"Part of being a duck is knowing how to swim," said Momma. "In a few years, you're not going to be able to depend on your Momma and your Poppa to protect you and to feed you. Someday you're going to have your own family, and you'll be responsible for finding food for all of your own little ducklings."

Buzzy just stared at his mother. "Now Buzzy, where do you think the best place is to find delicious little fish, green water weeds and your favorite bugs to eat?"

"Like the ones that Daddy brings home everyday?" asked Buzzy.

"Uh huh," said Momma Duck.

"Well, he just goes out on the pond and gets them," said Buzzy.

"Oh?" said Momma Duck, with a surprised look on her face. "On the pond? How do you get out on the pond to get those delicious little fish, green water weeds and your favorite bugs?"

"You've got to swim out there, Momma," said Buzzy.

All the little ducklings giggled and nodded at each other. They all knew that Buzzy was about to make a wonderful discovery. A great big smile appeared on Buzzy's face. Buzzy finally understood... "Momma, you're so wise. Now I understand why we are all out here every morning learning how to swim. You're really helping us to become independent ducks. Teaching us to swim is part of teaching us how to take care of ourselves."

The other ducklings just giggled and giggled.

They knew it all the time.

CHARLIE CHICKEN'S GREAT ADVENTURE

The Chicken family were a big family. There were always lots and lots of chicks around the Chicken house. Mama and Poppa Chicken had their hands full, tending to one family problem or another. By the time Poppa did his daily chores and climbed to the top of the barn to crow every morning, he was one tired old rooster. And Mama Chicken, sitting on all of those eggs every day and hurrying around the coop getting all of the chicks fed, was also very tired.

"Did all of you chicks brush your teeth, wash your hands and faces and change your clothes this morning? I don't want any of my chicks going to school with dirty hands and faces or wearing yesterday's clothes," she cackled.

"Yes Mama," they answered.

That is, all except... Charlie Chicken. "Who ever heard of a chicken brushing his teeth, washing his face and hands, and changing his clothes?" he mumbled to himself. "I'm just not going to listen. A Mother is not always right, and that's that!"

All of the Chicken children kissed Mama and Poppa goodbye as they went off to the barnyard school to learn how to scratch and peck, kick pebbles around and chirp, chirp, chirp the morning away.

But not Charlie. Charlie didn't want to go to school. Charlie was kind of an independent soul. Charlie always wondered what was really out there beyond the big brown fence that separated the barnyard from the rest of the world. Yes, Charlie was an adventurer. And so, Charlie decided to skip school and instead planned to slip away from the barnyard to have a look at the world outside. He packed his little bookbag with a days ration of Mama's delicious corn feed, an apple, and a few oatmeal cookies from the cookie jar. He took a bottle of his favorite Chocolate Cola and a little hat to shade his eyes from the afternoon sun, and off he went to see the world. Well, not the whole world, just the world outside the barnyard.

Charlie didn't tell Mama or Papa where he was going. He thought that he'd be home before supper and no one would ever miss him.

Once outside the big brown fence, Charlie crossed the dirt road that separated the barnyard from the rest of the world. He headed straight for the big field, the one filled with honeysuckle vines and clover.

"My, oh my, oh my! I'm finally out in the world on my own, with no one to tell me what to do. I don't have to brush my teeth. I don't have to wash my hands and face. I don't have to change my clothes. I don't have to do anything that I don't want to do. I can just sit here under this big old shade tree, smell the honeysuckle and clover and have a drink of my very own Chocolate Cola." And so it was.

But not for long, Charlie. Because at that very moment Farmer Brown's big shepherd dog Rex came trotting by. When Rex saw Charlie alone under that big old tree, he ran to the very spot where Charlie was sitting. "Woof, Woof, Woof!" barked Rex. "Who are you sir, and what are you doing under my tree?"

"Well, Mr. Rex," Charlie answered, "I'm Charlie, Mr. and Mrs. Chicken's son, and I thought it would be interesting to take a little trip and discover the world outside the barnyard."

"Ha, ha, ha," laughed Rex. "The world outside the barnyard is My world, and if you want to travel through it, you'll have to give me the rest of that Chocolate Cola."

Charlie thought quickly. "Well, why not? There's plenty of Chocolate Cola back home at the coop, so I'll just give the rest of my drink to Mr. Rex." And once again, Charlie was off to the see the world outside the barnyard.

The sun was high in the summer sky as Charlie hiked through another field of honeysuckle and clover. "Gee, it's getting close to lunch time," he thought. "I guess I'll stop here for a while, and snack on some of Mama's delicious homemade corn feed."

As Charlie sat enjoying his lunch, he thought to himself, "My, oh my, oh my! I'm finally out in the world on my own, with no one to tell me what to do. I don't have to brush my teeth, I don't have to wash my hands and face, I don't have to change my clothes. I don't have to do anything that I don't want to do." And so it was.

But not for long Charlie. Because at that very moment a big old buzzard spotted Charlie down below and came flying out of the sky very, very, fast, right to the very spot where Charlie was sitting. Charlie was really scared. The buzzard perched on a big rock just above Charlie's head, looked down at him with a nasty gleam in his eye, and said, "You are standing on my land, chicken, invading my privacy and disturbing the natural balance of the ecological system of this countryside. Now, what do you have in that bookbag that I can eat for lunch?"

Charlie was frightened. Except for the turkey family who lived in the barnyard, Charlie had never seen such a large bird before. "Just the rest of Mama's delicious chicken feed, an apple and some oatmeal cookies" Charlie answered.

"I'll take them," said the buzzard. And in the blink of an eye, the big bird flew off into the great blue sky and disappeared, taking the last of Charlie's food and leaving Charlie with nothing but an empty bookbag and his hat.

"Wow, that was close" thought Charlie. "Well, I've still got my hat to shade me from the afternoon sun." And off he went once again, to see the world outside the barnyard.

The afternoon sun was low in the sky as evening approached. Charlie was hungry. He wanted some of Mama's delicious corn feed or an apple with a cookie. "Wouldn't a Chocolate Cola taste wonderful about this time?" he thought. But the bookbag was empty. All of Charlie's food was gone. "Oh well, he thought, that's part of being an adventurer."

Charlie was an adventurer all right. Charlie was pretty brave, but right now, Charlie was lost. "Where am I?" he thought to himself. "I can't seem to figure this out. Sometimes I think that the barnyard is over there, and then I think that it's over here. Then I think that it's in some other place, but I'm not really sure. If I could only remember how I got here, maybe I would find the barnyard. Now, let's see. First I walked over that hill back there, then I crossed the stream and saw that big old tree, and then I met that nasty old dog named Rex, and then I walked through the field of clover below that snowcapped mountain and the buzzard flew out of the sky and took all of my food away. What will I do now? I didn't tell Mama or Poppa that I was off to see the world outside the barnyard. None of the Chicken children know where I am. Nobody knows where I am! I think that I'm just out of luck. I'm lost in the world. No one is ever going to find me. How can they find me? They don't even know where I have gone to. I should have listened to Mama and Poppa when they said, "Tell us where you are going, so that if you're not back on time we'll know where to look for you." "I was not too smart about this trip thought Charlie, not smart at all."

The stars and the moon gave off enough light for Charlie to see the way. He crossed a field, still recognizing the sweet smell of honeysuckle and clover. He passed one tree, then another that looked familiar, but still he was lost.

"Oh how happy I would be, just to see Farmer Brown's barn," thought Charlie. "I wonder what all of the chicks are doing right now?" Charlie was trying to keep his mind off his troubles. "They're probably all finished with dinner and doing their homework, or watching TV. I suppose Mama is knitting another sweater for one of the chicks and Poppa is probably fixing the screen door."

As day turned into night, the weather took on a chill that Charlie wasn't used to. At home, he would surely be snug as a bug in his own little bed, dreaming of the day when he would be old enough to leave the barnyard to explore the world. But now, all he could think of was where to rest and where to hide. He came upon a hollow log sitting out in the middle of the field, gathered enough grass and straw to cover his little body for the night, and crawled in. And as the moon and the stars hung high above in the nighttime sky, and the land was calm, Charlie fell asleep, lost in the world with no dinner tonight.

As the sun was rising on the second day of Charlie Chicken's great adventure. Charlie, deep in sleep, was still dreaming and reciting that tired old phrase: "My, oh my, oh my! I'm finally out in the world on my own, with no one to tell me what to do. I don't have to brush my teeth. I don't have to wash my hands and face. I don't have to change my clothes. I don't have to do anything that I don't want to do.

At that very moment in time, Charlie opened his eyes and jumped to his feet in an instant, still not believing what he was hearing. "Cockle Doodle Dooo, Cockle Doodle Dooo." "Why, I know that sound. That's my Poppa, crowin' from the top of the barn. Charlie was thrilled and excited. "Yahoo," he yelled.

Now all I have to do, is to follow that sound all the way home. "Cockle Doodle Dooo, Cockle Doodle Dooo." "What a beautiful sound," thought Charlie.

And so... down a slope, over the hill, through a wooded place next to a babbling brook, beneath a snowcapped mountain and over a field filled with honeysuckle and clover, Charlie followed his Daddy's call. By late morning he had crossed over the last clover field to the little dirt road that separated the barnyard from the world outside and as he walked along he could see Poppa Chicken standing proudly on top of Farmer Brown's barn singing his morning song. "Cockle Doodle Dooo."

Charlie learned a few lessons on this great adventure. I'll bet that he'll never look at the world outside the barnyard in the same way again.

Now Mama, she was angry. "Young man," she said. "You had every single chicken in this barnyard worried about you all night. The next time you decide to take a trip anywhere without telling your Mama or your Poppa where you are going, will be the last time you ever do anything by yourself.

"Yes m'am," said Charlie. Charlie was very glad to be home.

"Charlie," said Mama. "How was that great adventure of yours, anyway.?

"Well, it was ok, Mama."

Charlie didn't want to complain. He didn't want to tell Mama about that big dog named Rex who drank up all of his Chocolate Cola, or about that nasty buzzard who ate up all of his lunch. He didn't even want to tell Mama how hungry and cold and lonely he really had been.

"Well," said Mama. "Sit down and I'll make you a delicious breakfast. There's still half a day of school left, and I'm sure that all of the chicks will be happy to see you. By the way Charlie, why don't you take a bath, change out of those old clothes, brush your teeth and wash your face and hands before you go to school today? You know, you're not a baby chicken anymore."

BILLY AND BOBBIE BEAVER'S TRIP TO THE SUMMERTIME

Billy and Bobbie Beaver were brother and sister. They lived with their mother and father in a cozy Beaver Lodge (which is a house for beavers) in the middle of a pond, up stream from a very well constructed dam. Daddy Beaver built the dam and the Beaver Lodge all by himself. He built the lodge and the dam with mud and sticks and logs, which he chopped down with his enormously strong teeth. He gathered all of the building materials he needed very carefully. The job took most of the early spring and summer to finish.

The lodge had three entranceways. One was at the bottom of the pond in very deep water for the family to swim in and out of when the top of the pond was frozen over. The other two entranceways were on different sides of the lodge from which only a beaver family could enter and exit. This arrangement kept out all the other animals in the forest who wanted to do harm to the beaver family. There was also a kind of air vent on top of the lodge to let in fresh air and except for the chill that ran through the living area most of the year, (Mom used to call it nature's air condition-ing), it was really a cozy place indeed. A beaver family would never actually feel a chill in the lodge because they always had warm fur coats to wear. As the seasons changed, so would the thickness of their furs. As long as beavers ate the right kinds of food like mushrooms, pine nuts and red berries: chewed on tree bark and got the proper amount of exercise and rest, they would always be in the best of health.

At night, when it was real quiet in the lodge, Billy and Bobbie would lay in their warm beds and listen to the wind whipping around the trees, blowing away the last remaining leaves of summer; and from the air vent on top of the lodge they saw the first snowflakes fall. All of the animal families were safely in their places. The pond was calm. Every evening, as the sun rested its sleepy head in the west, the color of the season became a little more grey, until, as if overnight, winter had fallen upon the land.

"Brrr," said Billy to Bobbie as they gathered mushrooms, pine nuts and red berries. "It's very cold out here this morning. I miss the summertime when the breeze was warm and the days were bright and there were places to explore along the pond and I could be as lazy as I wanted to be." He explained. "Me too," added sister Bobbie. "And I miss making mud pies and snacking on poplar saplings and sweet summer berries. I wish that we could go somewhere else for the winter and come back to the beaver pond in the summer time," she said. "What a great idea," said Billy, as he swam through the icy cold water. "Race ya to the lodge," said Bobbie.

"You're on," replied Billy. And off they went. Beaver kids are all great swimmers.

Just then, Frankie Fox, appeared as if from out of nowhere. "Hi kids," he said through the foxiest smile that the Beaver kids had ever seen. "I have just come here to tell you that today is the opening day of my brand new travel agency. You can find it up the hill and around the bend. It's called The Foxy Travel Agency. We at Foxy Travel are selling trips to The Summertime."

"Trips to The Summertime?" said Billy. "What's that?"

"Well, every year about this time all of the critters who live around this wetland community, especially the younger ones, get to thinking about how nice it would be to leave this cold climate behind them and travel to a warmer place. A place that I call The Summertime. Now, let's see, there are the Grizzly Bear Cubs who live up in the cave on the hill, they want to go. The Rabbit Kids who live in the run, they're interested. And of course, the Squirrel Children who live in the big tree. Not to mention the Coyotes', the Owls' and the Hawks' Kids. They all would like to get away for the winter. So, if I can put it all together and get everybody to agree on this trip to The Summertime, would you be interested? It wouldn't cost but a few mushrooms, some pine nuts and some red berries." Frankie Fox, was a sly, sly Fox. Frankie Fox was not telling the truth.

"Sounds great," said Billy to Frankie Fox. "We'll go home to talk to Mom and Dad about it and call you with our decision."

"I'm sure that my Mom And Dad would just love to come along," said Bobbie. "My Mom and Dad really like the summertime best of all the seasons."

"One moment please," interrupted Frankie Fox. "I don't think that we should be discussing this trip with your mother and your father. This trip is only for younger critters." Frankie was lying again.

"You know, Frankie," Billy said. "You are right. If we're old enough to go hunting for mushrooms, pine nuts and red berries, I guess we're old enough to make our own decisions." Sister Bobbie nodded her approval. "Mr. Frankie Fox", said Billy. "My sister Bobbie and I accept your offer to go to The Summertime. When do we leave?"

Frankie was ecstatic. He couldn't believe his foxy furry ears. Visions of succulent beaver stew with mushrooms, pine nuts, and red berries kept dancing in and out of his head. The Fox family will surely make a hero out of Frankie Fox and a great feast out of those two plump little Beaver kids. "Right now," said Frankie, quivering with joy and delight. "There's a bus waiting right around the bend to take you to the, uh, to the uh," (Frankie was very excited, he could hardly speak.) "To the airport?" asked Billy. "Yes, Oh Yes! To the airport," answered Frankie.

At that very moment, Billy and Bobbie made one of the most foolish mistakes of their entire lives. They both walked out of the safety of the pond and on to dry land. And what's worse: Instead of remembering what Mom and Dad had taught them about not talking to strangers, they put their trust in a sly old fox.

Almost immediately, as if in the blink of an eye, two of the Fox brothers ran up behind the Beaver kids, and lickety split, threw a sack over each one. "Wow! that was easier than I thought it was going to be," said one of the Fox brothers. "We got us some fine beaver for supper."

"Hey", said Billy, "what kind of a game is this?" As he felt himself being lifted off the ground and thrown into the trunk of a car. Just then another sack came tumbling in on top of him. "Ouch!" said Billy, in a frightened voice "is that you, Bobbie?"

"Yes it is, Bobbie answered and I'm scared. We should never have believed that foxy old fox. We should have listened to Mom and Dad. What are we going to do now?" she asked.

Just then, the car came to a full stop. "Ah oh, I can hear someone walking over here," said Billy.

"Did you get 'em?" A strange foxie voice asked. "Did you get those two plump little beaver kids?"

"I sure did", said a very excited Frankie Fox.

"Good. Take them into the house and drop them into the cellar. I'll clean the mushrooms, pine nuts, and red berries, and tomorrow we'll prepare those two plump little beaver kids for the feast."

"Did you hear that?" whispered Billy. "Instead of a Trip to the Summertime, we're going on a trip to the supper table. We have to figure a way out of here, or else our goose is cooked!!"

Just then somebody opened the car trunk, lifted up the two sacks of beaver kids, carried them for a short distance and dropped them into the cellar. Kaplunk! kaplunk! They fell like sacks full of potatoes onto the bare earthen floor.

"Bobbie, Bobbie", whispered Billy. "I think that I can chew through this sack and so can you."

"Let's wait until it gets dark outside and maybe, just maybe, we might have a chance to escape," Said Bobbie.

When nighttime finally arrived, Billy and Bobbie chewed their way out of the sacks that had kept them prisoner all day.

"My goodness," said Bobbie, "we are being held prisoner in the foxes' cellar. All of the doors and windows have bars on them."

"Yes I know," said Billy. "Why don't you try to take a bite out of one of the bars on the cellar window?"

Bobbie laughed. "I know that we beavers have enormously strong teeth, but beavers can't bite through iron bars".

Billy giggled. "Well, why don't you just try to take a tiny little bite out of one those bars?"

Bobbie felt silly. "Ok, but only because you asked". Bobbie closed her eyes and wrapped her enormously strong beaver teeth around the bars. Crunch, crunch, "Mmm, this bar is delicious, and it's made out of wood. The paint is a little salty, kinda tastes like something that Mom prepared for dinner last week."

"Shhh," said Billy, putting his paw up to Bobbie's mouth and whispering into her ear. "Be a little quiet about chewing on this wood. We don't want to disturb the whole Fox family."

And so, as the moon and stars floated on high in the winter sky, Billy and Bobbie quietly did a little dance of joy, hoping that there was still a chance to get away from the Foxs' house before daybreak.

"Ok," whispered Billy. "I sure hope that everybody in the Fox family is fast asleep. Now Bobbie, you start chewing up all the bars on the windows and I'll start at the bottom of this door and the first one to make a hole large enough to crawl through is the winner." The contest began.

"I'm getting sick of chipping off all of this paint," whispered Bobbie.

"I'm sure that it doesn't taste as bad as this old door I'm chewing on," said Billy.

"Beavers forever," whispered Bobbie. "Beavers forever," replied brother Bill. They were determined.

They chewed and chewed all night long, leaving a huge pile of woodchips. Just before morning, Billy was able to crawl through a hole in the door. "I think that we can free ourselves from this cellar right now. We must be very careful not to wake anyone," said Billy.

They crawled out of the cellar door and hid in the high grass in back of the Fox's house. Billy could hear Frankie Fox snoring away through an open bedroom window.

"We have to get out of this place quickly," said Billy. Someone will surely wake up and try to recapture us." They waddled down the road as fast as their little feet could carry them.

At that very moment, Frankie Fox woke up. He walked over to the bedroom window and couldn't believe his eyes. "Do I see those fat little beavers' running down the road or am I dreaming? Hey, hey you! Beavers! Don't you want to go to The Summertime? Why are you running away?"

Frankie sounded the alarm to everyone in the house, "Beavers escaping, Beavers escaping," he yelled. And before you could say, "Beaver Stew," the whole family of foxes was on the road in their pickup trucks and motorcycles, searching for those two little runaway Beavers. Frankie also put the call out to all of the other critters in the forest. "Beavers on the loose, beavers on the loose. Come and get your wild beaver. We'll share in the feast with anyone who captures these two little wild creatures."

Of course, Frankie was lying again, but everybody in the forest knew that Frankie was a liar. Everyone except the Beaver kids. The Grizzly Bears came out to join the search. The Cougar family was there. The Wolf pack brought their friends, the Coyotes and the Wolverines. A couple of Hawks searched the sky and I think that the Eagle family were thinking about joining in the search. And, oh yes, the Owls were on the lookout as well. All to catch a meal of succulent, chubby, chewy, always fresh, Beaver Stew.

As Billy and Bobbie ran to the end of the forest, they could see the beaver pond right beyond the trees in the far meadow. The sun was just starting to rise and guess who was catching up to the fleeing Beaver kids? Yes, Frankie Fox on his motorcycle, was heading straight for them.

"Run, run" pleaded Billy, half out of breath.

"I'm doing the best I can," answered Bobbie. "I think that I ate too much wood last night. My stomach's too full to run any faster."

Frankie Fox rode up beside Bobbie. He tried to throw a sack over her head. She moved aside and the motorcycle kept rolling right along. "I'll get you on the turn around, Beaver," said that nasty old Frankie Fox.

Once again, Frankie turned his iron horse around and aimed it directly at Bobbie Beaver. Again she moved aside, dodging his attack, but this time, Bobbie turned only half way around and as Frankie Fox was approaching from another angle she crouched into a tiny little ball and whipped out her great big strong, shiny, slick tail, and as Frankie Fox came bearing down on her, Bobbie swung that tail around with all of her might, and boom!! She hit that sneaky Frankie Fox right in his foxy furry snout, knocked him clear off his motorcycle and sent him rolling down the mountainside.

"Hooray!" said Bobbie, dusting off her fur coat. "I just got me my first fox."

"Never mind your first fox," said Billy. "Let's try to figure out how to drive this motorcycle back home. I'm sure that every other critter in the forest would still love to make a meal out of us."

And so, Billy strapped on Foxie's helmet and goggles, and grabbed hold of the handlebars. Bobbie sat behind him and held onto Billy real tight, and down the mountainside they rode.

Papa was the first to see them from the rooftop window. "What are those crazy kids doing riding in the hills on a motorcycle? Don't they know that it isn't natural for a beaver to be riding a motorcycle?"

Mama Beaver chimed in. "Now Dad, kids will be kids"

Meanwhile, the Beaver kids parked the motorcycle in back of the dam. By then, every critter in the forest was just a few steps behind them. The chase was still, most definitely, on.

Billy grabbed Bobbie's paw and practically dragged her over to the dock on the pond. They were both breathing heavily as Billy turned to Bobbie and said, "Sister Bobbie, didn't we learn some important lessons in life today?"

"We sure did, Brother Bill. Race ya to the Lodge," said Bobbie.

"You're on," said Bill. "Beavers forever."

And into the water they went. Home for the winter.

PATTI PIG LOVES TO EAT

Patti Pig loves to eat. In fact, when she is not at the barnyard school where food is not allowed; you can always find her out back in the pig pen eating another meal.

Even though Mother Pig always reminds Patti to eat only three meals a day and to do her exercise, Patti never listens. Patti thinks that she knows better than Mother Pig.

Every morning, while all of the other animals are outside doing their daily exercise, guess where Patti is? You guessed it... Eating a second breakfast. She simply never gets tired of eating.

The horse family likes to gallop and trot around the barnyard in the morning. Galloping is very good exercise. Trotting keeps their bodies in good shape. All of the horses are proud of their healthy bodies.

The duck family waddles to the pond every morning and swims most of the day. Waddling and swimming is very good exercise. The duck family knows how important exercise is to good health.

All of the chickens and the goats and the dogs and the cows and the cats run and jump all over the barnyard. They are all in tip top shape.

But not Patti. She just doesn't care about staying in tip top shape. She never does exercise. As long as there is food around the pig pen, Patti Pig will surely eat it; and it's starting to show in the shape of her body.

One lunchtime, after treating herself to a very large portion of slop, grain and gruel, followed by an extra large dessert, Patti decided that the time was right to take a nice long nap in the mud. As the afternoon sun warmed the barnyard, Patti found a cool shady spot right in the middle of a mud patch in the shadow of the barn and settled in. "This world is truly a paradise for pigs," she thought. "All the food that I can eat, and all the sleep that I can sleep." And in the wink of an eye, Patti Pig was fast asleep.

Patti couldn't have been asleep for more than ten minutes before she opened her eyes to see a most interesting sight. "Why I do believe that I am floating in the air. If I didn't know any better, I could swear that I can just reach out and touch that big white fluffy cloud that's floating right by me. And oh! oh! I can touch it. Hey, I must be floating pretty high in the sky. I can see the whole world from up here. Isn't that the barnyard down below? And all of those teensy, weensy little animals, why they are all my friends. My goodness, there go the horses trotting around and isn't that the duck family swimming in the pond and aren't those goats and chickens, my very own school buddies, running and jumping up and down in the barnyard? And see all the cows walking to the barn. Oh, don't they look fine?

I can see dogs and cats running and playing with each other but they're getting smaller now. I must be floating higher and higher! Hey down there. Look at me! I'm a regular pink balloon, and I'm floating away. Can anybody hear me? Hey! Get me down from here."

But alas, nobody in the barnyard could hear Patti's cry for help. Who in the barnyard would ever think to look up into the sky for a missing pig anyway?

Time was slowly passing and Patti was flying higher and higher. So high, that she could no longer see her friends on the ground. "I wonder if I'll ever get back to the barnyard again" she thought. "How did my body ever get big enough to turn me into a great big pink balloon? I guess that it must have been all of that food that I have been been eating. I love my food. I can eat and eat and eat. But now that I'm floating away, I really can't think of eating another thing. I'm really sorry that I didn't listen to Mother Pig's advice. She told me to eat only three meals a day and to do my exercise, but instead I ate all day long and did no exercise. That's how I got to be this great big pink balloon that I am today. Well, from this moment on, I'm going to watch what I eat and do as much exercise as I can. In fact, I'm going to start exercising right now; and maybe, just maybe, I can get into some kind of shape and be lucky enough to float right back home to the barnyard.

Now let's see. The horses gallop, so I must move my legs just like a horse galloping. The ducks waddle and swim, so I must waddle from side to side and move my arms as if I was a duck swimming. The chickens flap their wings, so I must also make believe that I am flapping

17

my wings. The goats, dogs and cats run and jump all over the barnyard; so I'll just make believe that I'm doing their exercise as well.

And so, Patti Pig pretended to gallop like a horse, waddle and swim like a duck, flap her wings like a chicken, run and jump up and down like the goats, the dogs and the cats. What a sight she was! Patti Pig, right up there in the middle of the blue sky, galloping, waddling, swimming, flapping, and running and jumping. "I've got to get back to the barnyard," she said. "Just got to get back to the barnyard, I've got to get back to the barnyard. Just got to get back to the barnyard." Patti kept saying that same thought over and over again.

"Wake up Patti Pig," said the horse. "Wake up Patti Pig," said the duck. "Wake up Patti Pig," said the chickens. "Wake up Patti Pig," said the Cow. "Wake up Patti Pig," said the goats, and the dogs, and the cats.

"Why Patti Pig, you must be dreaming," said the horse. "You are back at the barnyard, and it's almost supper time. Why don't you wash your hands and face and join all of us for a delicious meal?"

Patti rubbed her sleepy eyes and looked up to see all of her barnyard buddies. The horses were there. The entire duck family was there. The chickens and the cows were there. All of the the goats and dogs were there. And oh yes, the cats, they were also there. All starring down at Miss Patti Pig and all of them with big smiles on their faces. Patti Pig was smiling too. She was really happy to be home again.

"Thank you all for asking," said Patti, "but I'm not very hungry. I've eaten enough food for today. See you all tomorrow morning for breakfast, and say, maybe we can all do our exercise together, before we go to school."

THE DREAMS OF WILLIAM GOAT

William Goat dreamed of being all grown up. He didn't want to wait until he finished school to be all grown up. He didn't want to wait until he was a bit taller or a bit stronger, or more experienced in life to be all grown up. He simply wanted to be all grown up.

William envied his older brother and older sister. They were all grown up. Every morning, as he dressed to go to school, his brother and sister would pack a lunch and climb aboard a bus to go off to work in the factory downtown. "They are so cool," thought William.

When William's older brother and older sister decided that they wanted to be all grown up, they simply quit school, and got a job. Working was really great fun for a while. They had enough money to buy all the things that they dreamed of having. Things like new clothing and new shoes. They had extra spending money to go to the movies. And what's more, they never had to read a book or do homework ever again.

Oh yes, it was great fun for a while, but they never really earned enough money to buy big items, like a house or a new car. So all in all, all that they had was a little extra pocket change and nothing more.

William earned almost as much money delivering groceries after school as big brother earned all week working at the factory.

Now, William's older brother wanted to marry his childhood sweetheart. But alas, they couldn't marry because big brother didn't have enough job security to support a family of his own. Oh, he was all grown up of course, and he did have a job. But then again, things like food and clothing were beginning to become quite expensive in town, and big brother really didn't know just how far his salary would go to support a future wife and child, house and car. Big brother began to wonder just what his future was beginning to look like. Oh yes, he could take a second job to help pay the bills, but that would mean not going to the movies on Saturday night and not buying new clothes and new shoes for a while. So he was back to where he started.

"Gee, you know?" said big brother. "If I didn't quit school, maybe I could have been trained to do a more responsible job at the factory. Maybe with a little more education I could have been making a better salary. Maybe I would be able to get married and buy a house and a car and have a family someday. Maybe I could really have the life that I dreamed about, now that I'm all grown up."

Sister had a similar problem. It seems that her boyfriend never completed his education either and was having difficulty finding a job. And so they too couldn't afford to get married, even though they were all grown up.

While it's true that they are all grown up; their future doesn't look too bright. They soon learned that going to the movies and buying an extra pair of shoes is definitely not the most important thing in life. What they are facing is an insecure future without a high school education, and close to no future at all without some kind of job training.

Soon, William began to understand that being all grown up had some serious responsibilities attached to it.

William was smart. After seeing and hearing the problem that his older brother and sister were having, he knew that he didn't want to face that same problem as well someday. And so, William decided that before he was all grown up, he was going to get a complete education and really prepare himself for whatever great adventure life has to offer. William knew that he could be anything that he wanted to be. He knew that all he had to do was to go to school and study hard to learn all about the subjects he would need when he grew up.

Some day, when William is all grown up, he will no doubt have all of the good things that a successful life has to offer.

It's really that easy when you start planning to be all grown up while you're still young.

BILLY'S RED WAGON

Problem Solving How To Ask The Right Questions How to Express Your Needs

Billy had a red wagon. It was all shiny and new. He was very proud of his red wagon. All the kids in the neighborhood enjoyed riding on Billy's red wagon. Billy shared his red wagon with everyone.

One day as Billy and his friends were playing with his red wagon, the weight of all the children broke the wagon in two places. "How am I ever going to repair my red wagon?" thought Billy. He was so confused.

Suddenly Billy remembered a lesson that he had learned in school. The subject was called: Problem solving. How To Ask The Right Questions.

If you have an idea about something, but can't figure it out, ask your teacher, ask your librarian, or ask a friend. Keep on asking until you get an answer. Make sure to get good information.

Billy took his broken red wagon to the local car dealer and asked if he could repair the red wagon. The car dealer looked at the broken wagon and said, "I can't repair this red wagon in my workshop, because I do not have the proper tools with which to fix it."

Billy was smart, he remembered to ask the right question to express his needs. "Mr. Car Dealer, said Billy. Who should I call to fix this broken red wagon?" The car dealer replied, "I think that a welder would be able to repair your red wagon. A welder is a person who can take two broken pieces of metal and heat them in a very hot fire until they get soft, and then press them together to make them look like one piece of metal again. You can find a welder in the yellow pages of the telephone book"

Billy was excited. He took his broken red wagon home and asked his mother to help him find the phone number of a welder in the telephone book.

Billy telephoned the Welder. "Sure enough," said the welder. "I have repaired many broken red wagons. Bring your red wagon to my shop tomorrow afternoon, and I'll have it repaired in no time at all."

And so, after school on the following day, Billy brought his broken red wagon to the welder's shop and watched as the broken red wagon was welded back together.

"Your red wagon is brand new again," said the welder.

"Thank you Mister Welder," said Billy. "I'm so glad that I learned how to ask the right questions to express my needs. I can do so much more now."

Barnyard Stories
Poems
By Artie Kaplan
Illustrations by Joe Toto

This portion of the book contains six original poems with illustrations for pre-school and elementary grade children. The illustrations are suitable for coloring. The poems, while entertaining, depict acts of unselfishness, compassion, humor and adventure.

One Little Green Frog
    Shows acts of unselfishness and heroism.

Two Little Honey Bears
Depicts humor and adventure.

Three Little Bunny Rabbits
Develops confidence and security

Four Little Kitty Cats
Is about the excitement of discovery.

Five Little Ducklings
Is about having fun and socializing.

Where Is Farmer Jones?
    Is a delightful poem that will capture the attention of children everywhere.

ONE LITTLE GREEN FROG,
MISTER FISH AND HIS DAUGHTER

One Little Green Frog, Mister Fish and His Daughter
By Artie Kaplan

One little green Frog
Sat upon a brown log
Bathing in the sun one day.

Resting his blue eyes.
Waiting for shoo flys
To fly out of a bale of hay.

Below in the water
Mister Fish and his daughter,
Were searching for their dinner as well.

And just as the shoo fly
Caught Mister Frog's eye,
The Frog reached for the fly and fell.

Kasplash went the water.
Scared off Fish's daughter.
As Froggy fell into the lake

A little embarrassed
And quite a bit harassed
The Frog gurgled, "give me a break."

Mister fish was excited.
His taste buds ignited.
This dinner he found was not planned.

All at once he gave chase,
To the frog, out of place.

Fish was now very much in command.

Just then a worm swam by
Caught Mister Fish's eye
She was wearing a grass hula skirt

Dancing and singing
Bucking and winging
While dishing up all of the dirt.
(From the bottom of the lake that is)

Well, Mister Fish lost his focus
And quick as hocus-pokus
The Green Frog just slithered away.

But the worm kept on dancing
And moving and prancing
Enough to make Mister Fish stay.

Just then from the bank
Frog saw fisherman Hank
Work his rod like he was close to a catch.

Frog jumped into the water
And found Fish's daughter
To warn her of father's bad match.

She said a quick thank you
And dove for the bank
You can bet she was there in a flash.

And just as that Wormy crook
Tried to slip Mister Fish "The hook"
His daughter jumped into the bash.

Daddy, daddy said daughter
Better do as I order
Don't you know worms like that break your heart.

First she'll tempt you, then hook you
Then someone will cook you
So let's go before troubles start.

Well, they flew through the water.
Mister Fish and his daughter
Back again to their home in the weed

Where they all lived happily ever after
Mister Fish, his Daughter and The Little Green Rafter.
Thanks to One Little Green Frog's good deed.

One little green Frog
Sat upon a brown log
Bathing in the sun one day.

Resting his blue eyes
Waiting for shoo flys
To fly out of a bale of hay.

Below in the water
Mister Fish and his daughter,
Were searching for their dinner as well.

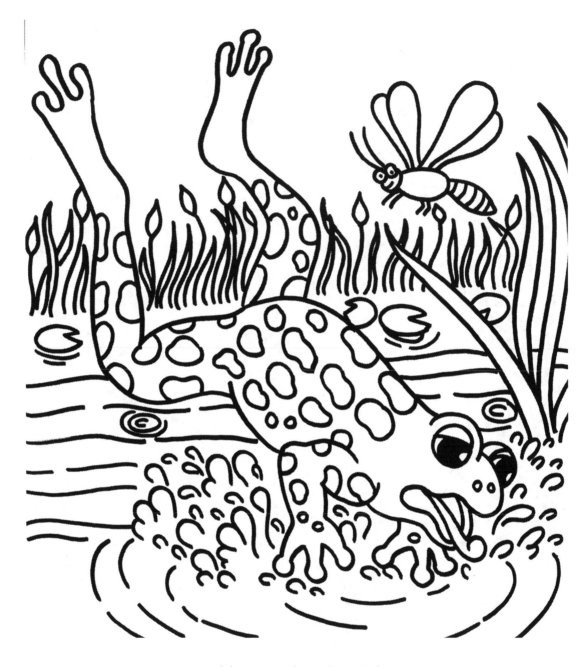

And just as the Shoo Fly
Caught Mister Frog's eye,
The Frog reached for the fly and fell.

Kasplash went the water
Scared off Fish's daughter.
As Froggy fell into the lake

A little embarrassed
And quite a bit harassed
The Frog gurgled, "Give me a break."

Mister Fish was excited.
His taste buds ignited.
This dinner he found
Was not planned.

All at once he gave chase,
To the Frog, out of place.
Fish was now very much in command.

Just then a worm swam by
Caught Mister Fish's eye
She was wearing a grass hula skirt

Dancing and singing
Bucking and winging
While dishing up all of the dirt.
(From the bottom of the lake, that is)

Well, Mister Fish lost his focus
And quick as hocus-pokus
The Green Frog just slithered away.

But the worm kept on dancing
And moving and prancing
Enough to make Mister Fish stay.

Just then from the bank
Frog saw fisherman Hank
Work his rod like he was close to a catch.

Frog jumped into the water
And found Fish's daughter
To warn her of father's bad match.

She said a quick thank you
And dove for the bank,
You can bet she was there in a flash.

And just as that Wormy crook,
Tried to slip Mister Fish "The hook"
His daughter jumped into the bash.

Daddy, Daddy said daughter
Better do as I order
Don't you know, worms like that break your heart.

First she'll tempt you, then hook you
Then someone will cook you
So let's go, before troubles start.

Well, they flew through the water,
Mister Fish and his daughter
Back again to their home in the weed

Where they lived happily ever after
Mister Fish, his daughter
And the Little Green Rafter
Thanks to one Little Green Frog's
good deed.

TWO LITTLE HONEY BEARS

Two Little Honey Bears
By Artie Kaplan

Two little honey bears, cute as can be,
Decided one day to climb up a tree.
So up they went, without a thought,
Of what they should and what they naught.

The first branch wasn't very high.
They could still see the ground,
On their climb to the sky
And so, they moved it up a bat
And on the second branch they sat.

"Why not," said they. It's just a tree
And so, they climbed to number three
And than to four and than to five
And soon they saw a honey hive.

The Honey Bees flew all about.
Each had a job to carry out.
They'd come and go from everywheres.
Paid no attention to the Bears.

Till Honey one said, "What a find"
There's so much honey here, I can't make up my mind.
And Honey two, was far from blue
You see, he had a sweet tooth too.

And so, Two Little Honey Bears
Proceeded to extract their shares.
But not for long and not for free
For soon, they angered every Bee.

Not one, not two, not ten, but all
The bees in the hive came to answer the call.
They swarmed around each Honey Bear
And stung them almost everywhere.

Yes, it was quite a sight to see
Two Honey Bears falling out of a tree
And running home to tend their bites
And lick their wounds through sleepless nights.

So heed this lesson, this lesson for sure.
If you learn it well, you will endure.

Before you decide to climb a tree
Look for the hive of the Honey Bee.
Even tho a Bee may be tiny and small,
One hundred Bees can be mighty and tall

And never take honey from a honey hive,
Unless you're prepared to be eaten alive.
If you don't believe me, well, pay me no cares.
Just remember the story of Two Honey bears.

And once you take what isn't yours
Better be prepared for the Honey Bee wars

Two little honey bears, cute as can be,
Decided one day to climb up a tree.
So up they went, without a thought,
Of what they should and what they naught.

The first branch wasn't very high.
They could still see the ground,
On their climb to the sky
And so, they moved it up a bat
And on the second branch they sat.

"Why not," said they. It's just a tree
And so, they climbed to number three
And than to four and than to five
And soon they saw a honey hive.

The Honey Bees flew all about.
Each had a job to carry out.
They'd come and go from everywheres.
Paid no attention to the Bears.

Till Honey one said, "What a find"
There's so much honey here, I can't make up my mind.
And Honey two, was far from blue
You see, he had a sweet tooth too.

And so, Two Little Honey Bears
Proceeded to extract their shares.
But not for long and not for free
For soon, they angered every Bee.

Not one, not two, not ten, but all
The bees in the hive came to answer the call.
They swarmed around each Honey Bear
And stung them almost everywhere.

Yes, it was quite a sight to see
Two Honey Bears falling out of a tree
And running home to tend their bites
And lick their wounds through
sleepless nights.

So heed this lesson, this lesson for sure.
If you learn it well, you will endure.

Before you decide to climb a tree
Look for the hive of the Honey Bee.
Even tho a Bee may be tiny and small,
One hundred Bees can be mighty and tall

And never take honey from a honey hive,
Unless you're prepared to be eaten alive.
If you don't believe me, well, pay me no cares.
Just remember the story of Two Honey bears.

And once you take what isn't yours
Better be prepared for the Honey Bee wars.

THREE LITTLE BUNNY RABBITS

Three Little Bunny Rabbits
By Artie Kaplan

Three Little Bunny Rabbits
Cozy and warm
Cuddled together
Safe from the storm

Mother Rabbit
Stays close by
Watching over
Her three small fry

Soon the clouds will go away
And morning will bring a brand new day

The sun will shine
While the Rabbits play
Jump in the grass and hide in the hay

The birds will sing
A summer song
And leaves on trees will sing along
While every golden daffodil
Will dance for joy upon the hill

It's such a special time of the year
For three little Bunny Rabbits
Who are finally here

Three Little Bunny Rabbits
Cozy and warm
Cuddled together, safe from the storm

Mother Rabbit
Stays close by
Watching over her three small fry

Artie Kaplan

Soon the clouds will go away
And morning will bring
a brand new day

The sun will shine
While the Rabbits play
Jump in the grass and hide in the hay

The birds will sing a summer song
And leaves on trees will sing along
While every golden daffodil
Will dance for joy upon the hill

It's such a special time of the year
For three little Bunny Rabbits
Who are finally here

FOUR LITTLE KITTY CATS

Four Little Kitty Cats
By Artie Kaplan

Four Little Kitty Cats fluffy and new
Took a stroll down the avenue.
Everything was big and tall
Oh, the wonder of it all

Cars and trucks were everywhere
On each street and thoroughfare
People walking to and fro
Traffic lights were all aglow

Giant signs on building tops
Selling giant ginger pops
Buildings reaching in the air

Through the clouds and through the glare
And they were there...four tiny things
If only Kitty Cats had wings

Even though they were so small
They'd fly on high above it all
But oh, when all is said and done

And truth be known to everyone
There's so much to look forward to
Four Kitty Cats are still brand new

Four Little Kitty Cats fluffy and new
Took a stroll down the avenue.
Everything was big and tall
Oh, the wonder of it all

Cars and trucks were everywhere
On each street and thoroughfare
People walking to and fro
Traffic lights were all aglow

Giant signs on building tops
Selling giant ginger pops
Buildings reaching in the air

Through the clouds and through the glare
And they were there...four tiny things
If only Kitty Cats had wings

Even though they were so small
They'd fly on high above it all
But oh, when all is said and done

And truth be known to everyone
There's so much to look forward to
Four Kitty Cats are still brand new.

FIVE LITTLE DUCKLINGS

Five Little Ducklings
By Artie Kaplan

Five little Ducklings, sleep in the straw.
Just beyond the old barn door
Open their eyes to see what they saw.
Five little Ducklings, sleep in the straw.

Five little Ducklings, wake up fast.
Morning hour is slowly past.
Days like this will never last.
Five little Ducklings, wake up fast.

Five little Ducklings, getting dressed.
They all want to look their best.
Now is not a time to rest
Five little Ducklings, getting dressed.

Five little Ducklings, take their places.
Eat their breakfast, wash their faces.
Some can even tie their laces.
Five little Ducklings, take their places.

Five little Ducklings, walk in a line.
Down to the pond, where the water is fine.
See them smiling. See them shine?
Five little Ducklings, walk in a line.

Five little Ducklings, love to play.
While the sun shines through the day.
"Please Mister sun don't go," they say.
Five little Ducklings, love to play.

Five little Ducklings, swim in a row.
Each one follows, where the other ones go.
See them rocking to and fro.
Five little Ducklings, swim in a row.

Five little Ducklings, having fun.
They like to swim with everyone.
Quack, quack, quack, till the day is done.
Five little Ducklings, having fun.

Five little Ducklings, fall asleep.
With nary a sound and nary a peep.
Close their eyes to see how deep.
Five little Ducklings, fall asleep.

Five little Ducklings, sleep in the straw.
Just beyond the old barn door
Open their eyes to see what they saw.
Five little Ducklings, sleep in the straw.

Five little Ducklings, wake up fast.
Morning hour is slowly past.
Days like this will never last.
Five little Ducklings, wake up fast.

Five little Ducklings, getting dressed.
They all want to look their best.
Now is not a time to rest
Five little Ducklings, getting dressed.

Five little Ducklings, take their places.
Eat their breakfast, wash their faces.
Some can even tie their laces.
Five little Ducklings, take their places.

Five little Ducklings, walk in a line.
Down to the pond, where the water is fine.
See them smiling. See them shine?
Five little Ducklings, walk in a line.

Five little Ducklings, love to play.
While the sun shines through the day.
"Please Mister sun don't go," they say.
Five little Ducklings, love to play.

Five little Ducklings, swim in a row.
Each one follows, where the other ones go.
See them rocking to and fro.
Five little Ducklings, swim in a row.

Five little Ducklings, having fun.
They like to swim with everyone.
Quack, quack, quack, till the day is done.
Five little Ducklings, having fun.

Five little Ducklings, fall asleep.
With nary a sound and nary a peep.
Close their eyes to see how deep.
Five little Ducklings, fall asleep.

WHERE IS FARMER JONES?

By Artie Kaplan

Illustrations by Joe Toto

Where Is Farmer Jones ?
By Artie Kaplan

The cow said moo
And the chicken clucked
And the pig said oink
While the quack quack ducked
And the sheep said baa
And the lamb said maa
Where is Farmer Jones?

And the cat meowed
As the dog bow wowed
While the horse just neighed
And the donkey breyed
And the bird went tweet
When the parakeet, said
Where is Farmer Jones?

Oh the mouse just shrieked
As the barn doors squeaked
And the faucet leaked
And the rafters creaked
And a goat jumped in
With a silly grin, said,
Where is Farmer Jones?

And the water rose
From that leaky hose
And where Farmer Jones is
Nobody knows
But he'd better come down
Before we all drown, say,
Where is Farmer Jones?

Oh the water's getting higher now
We're gonna get wet, not drier now
We'll soon go bust, run out of air
This isn't just, this isn't fair
And Farmer Jones isn't anywhere
So what is there to do?
Does anyone have a clue?

Who will come to save us now
Cluck said the chicken,
Moo said the cow,
Nee said the goat,
And baa said the lamb,
Does anyone have a battering ram
Can a pig or a horse send a telegram
While the water's rising
Can we build a dam
Does anybody have a better plan
Where is Farmer Jones?

Well I hear tell,
He's fast asleep
He's lost in dreams
And counting sheep
And pigs and chicks
And cows and goats
When he should be sowin' corn and oats
Instead, he's snoring away, they say
In the middle, In the middle,
In the middle of the day
When everybody else
Is bailing hay
And soon the barn will float away

Right off its cornerstones,
Say where, oh where, oh,
Where, oh where, oh,
Where is Farmer Jones?

The Cow Said Moo

And The Chicken Clucked

And The Pig Said Oink

While The Quack Quack
Ducked

And The Sheep Said Baa

And The Lamb Said Maa

Where Is Farmer Jones?

And The Cat Meowed

As The Dog Bow Wowed

While The Horse Just Neighed

And The Donkey Breyed

And The Bird Went Tweet

When The Parakeet, Said

Where Is Farmer Jones?

Oh, The Mouse Just Shrieked

As The Barn Doors Squeaked

And The Faucet Leaked

And The Rafters Creaked

And A Goat Jumped In
With A Silly Grin, Said,

Where Is Farmer Jones?

And The Water Rose
From That Leaky Hose

And Where Farmer Jones Is,
Nobody Knows

But He'd Better Come Down
Before We All Drown, Say,

Where Is Farmer Jones?

Oh The Water's Getting Higher Now

We're Gonna Get Wet
Not Drier Now

We'll Soon Go Bust, Run Out Of Air
This Isn't Just, This Isn't Fair

And Farmer Jones Isn't Anywhere

So What Is There To Do?
Does Anyone Have A Clue?

Who Will Come To Save Us Now?
Cluck Said The Chicken,
Moo Said The Cow

Nee Said The Goat,
And Baa Said The Lamb

Does Anyone Have A Battering Ram?
Can A Pig Or A Horse Send A Telegram

While The Water's Rising
Can We Build A Dam?

Does Anyone Have A Better Plan?
Where Is Farmer Jones?

Well I Hear Tell,
He's Fast Asleep

He's Lost In Dreams
And Counting Sheep

And Pigs And Chicks And Cows
And Goats

When He Should Be Sowin' Corn
And Oats

Instead, He's Snoring Away They Say
In The Middle, In The Middle,
In The Middle Of The Day

When Everyone Else Is Bailing Hay

And Soon The Barn Will Float Away
Right Off Its Cornerstones,

Say Where, Oh Where,
Oh, Where, Oh Where, Oh,
Where Is Farmer Jones?

Barnyard Stories
and poems
By Artie Kaplan

This book contains six original stories and six poems designed to make young children aware of traditional values. Through the circumstances and situations of the animal characters in these Barnyard Stories, children can relate their own concerns and experiences.

Each story and poem teaches a valuable lesson.
Buzzy Duck's   Wonderful Discovery: About understanding the importance of independence and responsibility.

Charlie Chicken's Great Adventure: About acting on your emotions and then realizing what is really important.

Billy And Bobbie Beavers' Trip To The Summertime: While it is fun to dream, learning who to trust is more important.

Pattie Pig Loves To Eat: Pattie learns the value
of good health habits and proper exercise.

The Dreams Of William Goat: William learns the importance of being patient in preparation for his lifetime goals.

Billy's Red Wagon: Is a lesson in learning to ask the right questions to find solutions.

One Little Green Frog: Shows acts of unselfishness and heroism.

Two Little Honey Bears: Depicts humor and adventure.

Three Little Bunny Rabbits: Develops confidence and security

Four Little Kitty Cats: Is about the excitement of discovery.

Five Little Ducklings: Is about having fun and socializing.

Where Is Farmer Jones?: Is a delightful poem that will capture the attention of children everywhere.

An audio CD of the author reading the enclosed stories and poems is available for this book. Consult our website: AKPRecords.com, email us at: awk@airface.com, or write for a price list to: AKP Inc., PO Box 4008, Deerfield Beach, FL 33442

ABOUT THE AUTHOR

Artie Kaplan is a robust, friendly and fun loving guy. He is the kind of person that every little boy and girl would like to have as a real or imaginary friend.

His songs and stories about real and imagined happenings leave children spell bound and delighted. Sometimes with a lesson learned, and sometimes, "just for the fun of it." There is always an underlying message that subtly imparts important universal values regarding children's' relationships with other people and the world in which they live.

Kaplan has been associated with the music industry for over forty years. As a musician during the 60's, 70's, and 80's, Artie Kaplan appeared on many hit singles and albums recorded by the leading recording artists of the era.

As a songwriter, producer and Music publisher, Artie Kaplan wrote and produced the music for Metromedia's "Wonderama" television show, a Sunday morning favorite among children. Some of the more memorable songs from that show were "Kids Are People Too", and "Oh Gee It's Great To Be A Kid," both titles being the theme song of the show at various times in its development. Artie has also produced a number of recordings of international acclaim. "Harmony" and Bensonhurst Blues" stand out among his best work. His songs also appear in several films as theme songs.

Most recently Artie Kaplan has changed his direction from popular music to creating beautiful songs and stories for and about children and their situations.

What emerges from Artie Kaplan's writings is the devilish little boy who was in us in our youth and is still within Artie Kaplan today.

"Barnyard Stores And Poems" is but one of Kaplan's recent creations.